READING POWER

Grant Hill
Basketball All-Star
Rob Kirkpatrick

The Rosen Publishing Group's
PowerKids Press ™
New York

1

For my nephew, Cameron. (I'm undefeated against you.)

Published in 2000 by The Rosen Publishing Group, Inc.
29 East 21st Street, New York, NY 10010

First Edition

Book design: Michael de Guzman

Photo Credits: p. 5 © Ezra Shaw/Allsport; pp. 7, 11 © Jonathan Daniel/Allsport; p. 9, 17 © Scott Cunningham/NBA Photos/Allsport; p. 13 © Noren Trotman/NBA Photos/Allsport; p. 15 © Allsport USA; p. 19 © Phil Sears/Allsport; p. 21 © Doug Pensinger/Allsport; p. 22 © Jed Jacobsohn/Allsport.

Text Consultant: Linda J. Kirkpatrick, Reading Specialist/Reading Recovery Teacher

Kirkpatrick, Rob.
    Grant Hill : basketball all-star / by Rob Kirkpatrick.
        p. cm. — (Reading power)
    Includes index.
    SUMMARY: Introduces the former Duke University basketball star, Grant Hill, who now plays for the Detroit Pistons.
        ISBN 0-8239-5538-9
        1. Hill, Grant Juvenile literature. 2. Basketball players—United States Biography Juvenile literature. [1. Hill, Grant. 2. Basketball players. 3. Afro-Americans Biography.] I. Title. II. Series.
        GV884.H45 K57 1999
        796.323'092—dc21
        [B]   99-16002
                                                           CIP

Manufactured in the United States of America

Contents

Grant Hill plays basketball.
He is in the NBA.

Grant plays for the Detroit Pistons. He is number 33 on the Pistons.

Grant can dribble the ball well. He can run fast, too.

Grant can make baskets to get points. Grant gets a lot of points for his team.

Grant can dunk the ball.
He can dunk the ball with
one hand.

13

Grant is a good passer.
He likes to pass the ball.
He can pass the ball with
one hand.

Grant plays good defense.
He stops the other team
from getting baskets.

17

Grant played basketball in school. He played for Duke. Duke's team was called the Blue Devils. He was number 33 for Duke.

19

Grant helped Duke win a lot of games. When they won a big game, Grant got to cut down the net.

In 1996, Grant played in the Olympics. He played for the United States.

Here are more books to read about
Grant Hill:

Grant Hill: Smooth as Silk (Sports
Stars)
by Mark Stewart
Children's Press (1999)

Grant Hill
by Paul Joseph
Abdo & Daughters (1998)

To learn more about basketball, check
out this Web site:

http://www.nba.com/

Glossary

dribble (DRIH-bul) When a player bounces the ball on the floor.

dunk (DUNK) When a player reaches up and drops the ball right into the basket.

Olympics (oh-LIM-piks) Games where the best athletes in the world compete.

pass (PAS) To throw the ball to a player on the same team.

Index

Word Count: 149

Note to Librarians, Teachers, and Parents

If reading is a challenge, Reading Power is a solution! Reading Power is perfect for readers who want high-interest subject matter at an accessible reading level. These fact-filled, photo-illustrated books are designed for readers who want straightforward vocabulary, engaging topics, and a manageable reading experience. With clear picture/text correspondence, leveled Reading Power books put the reader in charge. Now readers have the power to get the information they want and the skills they need in a user-friendly format.